I0499727

OVERCOMING THE DISTRACTION ADDICTION:

THRIVING WITH PRODUCTIVITY THROUGH

FOCUS

A complete strategy to do less,
achieve more & live a better life.

by

David Turner

Copyright © 2019 by David Turner

ISBN: 9781706954118

All Rights Reserved.

No part of this publication may be reproduced in any form or by any means, including scanning, photocopying, or otherwise without written permission of the copyright holder.

First Printing, 2019

Summary of the Book:

Your ability to focus and eliminate distraction is one of the most important skills that are necessary for progress and success in your life. The higher your ability to focus, the more quickly you can complete a task, which would result in a considerable change in your life. The first step is to understand what distraction is and how it can negatively impact your life and career.

Everyone gets distracted irrespective of who you are, and it affects the way we think and act. However, without focus, distractions can turn into a full-fledged habit which can negatively impact on your productivity. Attention implies singularity in what you do. Focusing on one thing is very difficult, but it is the key to achieving success in your life.

You need to adopt effective strategies to get rid of distractions. Time, training, and commitment are required to keep your focus. Training the mind to maintain its focus takes a lot of effort, but they are worth it. Taking a break and avoiding multitasking are a real handful of strategies to relax your body and avoid distractions. Once you minimize distractions, you would begin to realize so many opportunities in what you do.

Focus helps you to understand the importance of the task at hand and give it your utmost best. Focus can generate a great result for you, which would lead to your success. It is important to understand that so many people have failed as a result of distraction. They jump from one distraction to another without maximizing the opportunities in what they do.

Overview of what the book has covered:

- Learning about distractions and how it transforms into an addiction
- Brain Refining for Less distraction
- The mind exercise for maximum focus
- Minimizing distraction through a healthy lifestyle
- Procrastination a pathway to distraction.
- Effectiveness of Planning & Scheduling
- Break as a key instrument for better focus.
- The powers of meditation
- Proper hydration for Body refreshment
- Power of focus for more
- Importance of focus for better time management.
- Learning from mistakes through better focus.

"Don't get taken captive by distractions, focus your way to freedom"

* * * * *

"The successful warrior is the average man,
with laser-like focus."

Bruce Lee

* * * * *

"That's been one of my mantras – focus and simplicity.
Simple can be harder than complex:
You have to work hard to get your thinking clean to make it
simple. But it's worth it in the end because once you get there,
you can move mountains."

Steve Jobs

* * * * *

"You don't get results by focusing on results.
You get results by focusing on the actions that produce results."

Mike Hawkins

Table of Contents

CHAPTER 1:

DISTRACTION IS AN ABYSS

Modern life comes with a plethora of distractions on a daily basis to the point that it becomes difficult to maintain consistency. The only solution is to fight on and try your best to break free from the dungeon your mind is trapped in. It may drag you to a state of complete mental distraction and can be extremely harmful as far as your performance is concerned. The harm can be more lethal than you have ever imagined it to be. Once you are trapped in a deep dark borderless chasm called 'distraction' you actually postpone living your life.

Distraction is in a way mental distress that blocks an individual's ability to complete the tasks at hand. It goes without saying that you have to force your mind not be distracted and smoothly carry on with your daily tasks. You have to tell your mind constantly that you have to get through in any way possible.

Honestly speaking, all of us face distractions in many forms every day but it's how we take our destructive tendencies and how we execute our actions that matter. The way we classify our distractions makes a difference in how to find a solution to this dilemma. Whether they are internal or external, emotional or professional, fears or worries, we have to be fully aware of our conscience.

It doesn't matter how you classify the different types of distractions which are commonly divided into three stages like Visual, Manual, and Cognitive. According to professionals, the contemporary technological involvements and dependence in our lives is one of the core destructive elements. These can be further elaborated as the Internet, Smartphones, Social Media, Emails & Digital Correspondence, Noise of every kind by these digital machines. Further, the distractions created by co-workers, Multitasking, Micromanagement of every little thing that goes about in your lives.

In other words, you have to stop complicating your life and start putting yourself back on track by simply avoiding the distractions that intermingle with procrastination and every other bad habitual tendency you are facing.

Is a Distraction an Addiction?

Is Distraction an addiction?

Do we reach a state where we find ourselves addicted to being distracted which is merely a disruption to complete a job we have been assigned for? Or is it a creative healthy coping mechanism for most of you? This point is critical to understand because that is where we lose the ability to identify how badly this addiction is hurting us. Smartphones have been declared as a major disruptive factor as we keep on procrastinating and failing to maintain a balance. These digital devices can cause an immense amount of distraction to derail you to delay scheduled tasks which may be the most important way forward in your professional or personal growth.

Is it a Habit?

Is it a Habit?

Distractions may become your habit if you repeatedly prolong such habits unconsciously. In fact, habits are what make an individual what he or she stands for. When you repeat your actions constantly for a particular span of time it becomes your habit whether it is good or bad. That's how distractions become part of your routine life and you don't even notice it. It derails your focus and hurts your productive life.

Is it a Stress Reliever?

Sometimes it plays a positive role to distract you from the hectic workload and busy schedule you are coping with. In such a scenario, being distracted does seem positive. It feels good to have a nice break where you can listen to your favorite music, watch a TV show, and do everything that solely makes you feel good about yourself and your surroundings. It freshens you up and makes you forget about the intense work routine you have to face every day.

Our Brain, a Battlefield of Thoughts:

Our brain is a battlefield of the thoughts.

Good or bad thoughts are constantly having a tussle in your brand. What you have to do is to train your mind to beat the bad thoughts but beat them with complete authority. Clouding your mind with negative thoughts is never good for both your physical and mental wellbeing. The only way you can outweigh such daunting thoughts is to fight them off with a positive attitude but with consistency.

Don't Feed It:

Distractions grow like a sycamore as you shower them with useless disruptions and disarray; you have to stop feeding them as simple as that. As you feed them with negative or unwanted thoughts they multiply like a virus and disturb every aspect of your life.

As you indulge in distraction, you tend to procrastinate a lot. You keep on feeding the bad habit of yours without realizing how harmful it can be. To the extent, that it can shatter your dreams and ambitions. It damages your day-to-day life; it stops you from living your life to the fullest. It also makes you lose your capacity to cope with daily issues. You may fail to keep the best of your usual self as you soon feel your integrity starting shrunken.

Most of the time it seems impossible to stay focused on the task, further it can be very challenging when there are constant distractions around. The world we are living right now is full of distractions. Even in peaceful and quiet places, we can be distracted by mere applications installed in our smartphones. Because we end playing some random online games to pass off time.

Schedule Your Tasks:

Schedule Your task.

It is always good to plan your day and schedule your working hours as precisely as you want. Divide and distribute your working hours smartly as per the need of your task. It is a roadmap to achieve the daily tasks you have set for yourself and your workers. Planning and organizing keep you focused because you can be distracted easily if you have not planned how to streamline your productivity.

Sleep is Always Good:

Sleep is always good.

Always have enough sleep since it is not only good for your health but also lets you work with full efficiency. In fact, a good sleep prepares you for the day ahead of you. It relieves mental fatigue and physical tiredness; you can re-energize yourself after getting rest you deserve after a long tiring day. You can do several things to get proper sleep if you fail in doing so. You can commence with doing a quick and easy exercise which can help you find the sleep you lost.

Eat Healthily

Eat Healthy

Eating healthy food makes your body and mind fit to tackle everyday tasks and lets you prepare you for the hectic workday right ahead of you. It helps you work long hours to rejuvenate your lost energy and the burnouts you feel. Modern studies suggest there is an integral link between your food habits and working abilities. If you want durable energy daily to face on your chores you have to adopt healthy food habits. For example, excessive use of junk food, heavy intake of sugar or salt makes you lethargic and your body easily feels fatigued in a very few hours of the day. It kills your productivity and even a normal course of workload would be difficult for you to finish.

Eating habits at home and workplace are essential when you are seeking high performance in a limited time assigned. Nowadays it is not very difficult to acquire good healthy food, you can find ready to eat organic food almost everywhere. The point is are you ready to quit the junk food you already addicted to. It is also not as difficult if you want to prepare healthy food for yourself at home there are a surplus of online recipes available on different websites. The only effort required from your end is to just have to fetch the ingredients and take time to prepare meals for yourself.

Distractions Are Not Always Negative:

Positive distractions can be helpful for your efficiency to complete tasks as several studies have proved that when you exposed workers with a different kind of distractions, their reaction is either positive or negative. And the positive distractions do not interfere with the routine of the workers. In fact, it increases their performance whereas negative distraction makes them slow or dull while finishing their job.

Listening to soothing music and performing meditation will always help you re-gather your energy and regain your focus, but on the other hand, plain noise or smartphone notifications or your emails always distract you and kill your drive to work.

Tailor Your Time According to Your Habits:

Tailor your time according to your habit.

Are you a day-person or are you nocturnal? You know yourself better than anyone else. Choose your working hours according to your habits. If you think you are more of a Day-Person do the major workload in the first half of the day so that you can do it wholeheartedly. If you think you are nocturnal, choose your work hours accordingly. Your habits of adopting work at different times of day can be vital to your performance, so it is advisable to do it as your habits of work are convenient for you.

14

Handling multiple tasks diverts concentration and you are not able to show the best of you. Attention always helps, it helps you focus and produce quality work. When you try to indulge in multitasking you end up with unnecessary repetitions that kill the quality of your work. For example, you are writing for a blog or journal and along with you have been assigned some work of SEO Marketing this is definitely going to compromise the quality of your content.

Co-workers and their attitude toward their work are very important. If you have a friendly and supportive co-working space, you find it easy to produce better work with complete composure. It has also been observed that conducive co-working spaces make workers more comfortable to spend their productive hours in comparison with working spaces which unfriendly and unwelcoming.

Announce it, 'You are Busy':

Announce it you are busy.

You have to let every person at your workplace know that 'you are busy', make it clear and loud to everyone that you should not be disturbed. That's how important your work is to you. Ensure to make it a routine so that you can avoid useless and avoidable intervention by your fellow workers. Gossips and interactions which are not related to work stop you from performing to your fullest, everyone should have a complete realization that your work is the most important thing when you are at your workplace.

Negative people whether they are at your workplace or in your social circle should be stopped spreading negativity, you should avoid them in the first place. Secondly, you should restrain yourself from hanging out with them because while they may not be putting themselves in a dark spot, but they will be putting your creativity and productivity at risk.

You should strive to include positive people in your social circle who can appreciate your work and small gestures; inclusion of good company can boost your confidence and help you focus on what's important.

You have to fight back every time when internal and external distractions slow you down. Be an early riser and plan your day. Start your day with positive energy because it is going to last long until the day ends. Be simple and be prepared for every trial that comes in your way. Pinpoint the clutter that is making you out of focus.

Clear your mind with positive energy, have healthy food and prepare yourself for everyday distractions because you have to face them anyway. Be calm and make yourself comfortable, this way you can tackle your thoughts comprehensively. Do not hide away from your issues instead point them out and find solutions with a positive attitude.

Regular meetings at your workplace waste a lot of time when that time can be utilized in increasing productivity and efficiency. While you should not avoid such small meetings at your workplace, you can always find a better alternative to the time spent in the meeting. Once it ends, you should embark on a productive activity.

CHAPTER 2:

TRAIN YOUR BRAIN TO FOCUS

* * * * *

"Person who chases two Rabbits catches neither"

Confucius

You have to train your brain to focus and tame it to do the things that you perceive. The fear and pressure in your life can leave you unfocused; this kind of behavior has been called 'Monkey Mind' by the psychiatrists. As you keep reading, you'll understand that training your mind is the same as locking that money in its rightful cage.

How Distraction is Nothing but Negative:

How Distraction is Nothing but negative.

Ever wondered why you never get to achieve great marks in a test, while others are able to do easily? It is for sure that you're not focusing on the right things, but the main reason is that your mind isn't at rest. Even when you feel like that you might be doing well in life; the monkey mind doesn't display kindness for everyone. Suffering from a distracted mind is the same as being paralyzed in your sleep and unable to tackle the dark hands that crawl by the side of your bed. But as you wake up from the nightmare, you thank reality that the miserable experience was nothing but an image on your part. Though, is it really that easy for anyone to break out of the toxic shell that a distracted mind puts them in? The simple answer is no as if it were that easy, almost everyone would have never complained about procrastinating. None of the hot-shots or owners of multi-millionaire companies would have been able to achieve and brag about their achievements, without constantly avoiding distraction. This is why it is so awe-striking seeing these successful people and thinking to yourself, "How were they able to give their utmost focus to this particular cause?" you must've thought about starting your own business, launching a clothing line, or even opening an art gallery, but your focusing capacity just won't cooperate. There are so many things that you need to look into, which include spending time with loved ones, studying, or getting a job. But you overburden yourself heavily with these tasks and are unable to display productivity in any of them. It is the same as chasing after some papers that have flown into a river. You end up panicking over how you're going to get into the waters and grab the papers. And once you jump into the river, you can see that the papers are scattered everywhere. So you confuse yourself as you try to pick up all of them. In the end, you give up on collecting the papers because you got overwhelmed and decide to march home. What happened here? You just lost your focus and ended up riding on the waves of panic that the situation bestowed on you.

An Unfocused Mind Procrastinates:

An Unfocused Mind Procrastinates

Another thing that a distracted mind provides is the unasked, annoying concept of 'procrastination'. It is for sure that procrastination in itself is a major consequence of a distracted mind as you barely find the motivation to complete a task. The reason why we indulge in hopeless activities and divert away from the real deal is that we know the necessary task is significant. However, our brain and body convince us that leaving the comfort zone is stressful; it leaves our heart pounding in our chest. And that is undeniably natural because every person diverts away from productivity at least once a week. It isn't a concept that we should be punishing ourselves for. But that does not mean that we shouldn't figure out a solution for it as well. Moreover, a professor specializing in procrastination in Carleton University mentions that people become anxious while working on a significant task. This means that the constant pressure on them compels them to lose 'interest' in the task as they fear that feeling might come back. So, they end up becoming distracted. This is the same situation as the paper incident. You just become anxious because of the hefty task, which intrigues you to run away and get distracted as a result.

This brings us to the connection between negativity and distraction. When your mind is swinging from one thought to another, it becomes easy to shift towards the negative thoughts rather than the positive ones. "I feel too tired right now" or "I need to clean my room" such excuses are actually negative thoughts that you convince yourself of just to stay out of completing work. This is because humans are, often, wired towards the bad as we tend to look at our mistakes and flaws with more strictness. Even research mentions that people prioritize and dwell more over the negative experiences as we tend to learn and grow from them. It is always the pessimistic experiences in our lives that stand out to us and determine our future steps. Considering that this is a natural process, anyone that suffers from negativity is a normal human being. Positivity and negativity are like Yin and Yang, as one cannot survive without the other. However, is that really an excuse for a person to keep making themselves miserable by overthinking or having unnecessary thoughts? The only thing that can act as a 'magic potion' for you in this scenario is the idea of focus.

How To Keep Your Mind Focused:

How to keep your Mind focused.

It isn't easy to train your mind in a way that you know it would listen to you. However, the process is necessary because everything that you want to achieve depends upon whether you stay focused or not. So, here are a couple of tips to sharpen your mind, and transform it from a rusted dagger to a glistening katana:

Don't Shy Away from Planning:

Don't shy away from planning.

Planning out a task is possibly the best thing that you can do before performing it. One of the reasons why people are distracted is because they don't know how to commit to a task or achieve it. They don't plan it out properly and become overwhelmed when they see the number of things that they have to cater to. Often, they even end up planning out the task in their head but as they get to it, they forget the sequence. This is why you need to write, write, and write. You should be making notes about how you will be achieving a task. For example, James is a new writer who has recently been provided with a writing task. He starts to work on it, but he doesn't plan out the article.

20

Eventually, he writes a paragraph but realizes that he suffers from a writer's block in the middle. This is because he did not divide the article into specific parts, nor did he do any research. He didn't know which sub-heading should've goes well with which part of the article. And soon he becomes stuck in the middle of writing.

* * * * *

"Failing to Plan is Planning to Fail"

* * * * *

So, before performing any task, either studies or work-related, plan it out in your head but word it out as well. As you look at the organized sequence, you don't pressurize yourself and remain focused on the task on hand. Another thing to consider is the sudden urge to procrastinate. To tackle that, all you have to do is think about the refreshing feeling that will engulf you when you complete the task. When you start enjoying the success that you receive after achieving something, you won't direct yourself towards lazing off in the first place. Lastly, it is all about envisioning positivity rather than dwelling over the fact of, "would I be able to complete this on time?" try to be less harsh on yourself and visualize the good outcomes only. However, that doesn't mean that you display unprofessionalism at the workplace or do not complete homework at the given deadline. It is about caring for your health and knowing your limits. You can only be able to focus when you are not straining yourself to achieve something but rather knowing the optimistic side of a situation.

Give Up Multi-Tasking – Focus on One Thing at A Time:

Our generation is fixated on multitasking because of its productive nature of getting more than one thing done. However, a lot of us don't realize that we are completing tasks with less efficiency.

When it comes to participating in more than one task, it becomes difficult to achieve the same results for both. So, in the end, you just have to compromise on one.

This is also why a lot of companies or workplaces are trying to remove constraints on their employees, ensuring that the employees give beneficial results. See, if you're working in an environment where you have to prepare fifteen documents for a marketing team. While you also have to sketch a business plan, do you think you would be able to function normally? It would chew away from your attention until you become a living skeleton staring at a screen just contemplating how to even type.

If you give one thing your absolute focus, then you juice out better results because the entire day that is your only priority. Instead of being greedy, try to be lenient on your capabilities.

Take a Short, Well-Deserving Break:

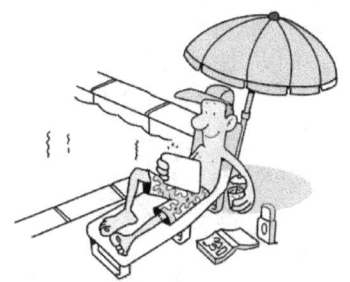

Take a short, Well deserving break

Breaks are always emphasized because it is impossible to achieve something without having to restart your thoughts. When you tend to a task for too long, you can realize that your attention span is simply slipping away. It is the same as reading a book and continuously reading one paragraph because you are feeling too tired to make sense of the words. During this time, if you put the book down and make yourself a fresh glass of banana milk, then you give yourself time to regain your focus back.

It doesn't matter if that break is for a couple of minutes, but it is very much required for better productivity. Though, don't use the break as a method to divert your mind away from the original task. This brings us back to the planning part, as you should even plan some of the breaks that you might require in between. Try to figure out the hours of each break, so that the 'overwhelming' feeling doesn't take over to compel you to procrastinate.

Dwell into The Peaceful World of Mindfulness, Meditation or Prayer:

If it didn't seem obvious enough, meditation and prayer are also a great option to collect your thoughts and improve focus. Research has proved that meditation and prayer help uplift the attention span and inject calmness in a person's system. Moreover, you don't even need to spend an hour or so on meditation or prayer; studies say that only 10 to 20 minutes suffice as well. Basically, mindfulness meditation is the ultimate method of quieting the storm in your head and only focusing on generically relaxing things. This includes picturing a waterfall in the back of your head and just not letting your focus diverted away from that. If you ever feel a thought other than this coming to your head, then you just ignore it.

Dwell into the peaceful world of the mindfulness or meditation

However, if you are unable to do so then you need to ask yourself, why exactly do you keep having that thought? Why is it that hard for you to ignore this particular thought? It is perfect for evaluating what concerns you and focusing on your present rather than anything else. And you can practice it in any setting, for example you can be mindful while swallowing food and tasting the flavors as the food slides down your throat or while turning a page in a book and feeling the sensation of the paper under your fingertips. You can even focus on your own breath to calm down and just feel yourself in the present moment. A lot of us don't realize the significance of the current moment because we are so obsessed with our surroundings. It is almost like we have romanticized the concept of being busy. When we are not busy or stressing out, we feel that we are not being productive or not thinking about our future. It is the same for when we blame ourselves for a past event and lose our focus while obsessing over things that have already passed. Hence, it is important to focus and appreciate the present as that helps dust off any burdening thoughts and serves as an encouraging push to the back.

Nevertheless, of all these tips, you need to remember that moving away from your comfort zone and training your brain to focus, is hard. It is a lengthy, strenuous process that isn't achievable in a couple of weeks. You need to be patient and trust yourself throughout the training session. In the end, you're the one who is in charge of your own mind, so you have to fix it. Therefore, make sure to not stress yourself and just allow yourself to move with the flow.

CHAPTER 3:

THE BEAUTY OF PRODUCTIVITY

The difference between successful people and the ones who are struggling to be successful is that a successful individual maintains his productivity by overcoming distractions of all sorts.

You have to increase focus by doing small things, in the words of Confucius 'Person who chases two Rabbits catches neither', you have to train your brain to focus or you have to tame your brain to do things you have perceived. Fear and pressure in life make your vision out of focus; this kind of mind behavior has been called the 'Monkey Mind' by psychiatrists, a term borrowed from Buddhist principles. The goal is to not only train your mind to avoid unnecessary thoughts but also to lock the monkey in your mind into the rightful cage so that your mind is solely under your control.

By indulging in multiple thoughts at once, you lose focus and only doubts and negative thoughts take over your mind. That, in turn, affects your mindfulness and productivity. The time you learn to calm down your monkey mind you steer your life away in total control.

Meditate to Increase Focus:

'Meditation is the primary way to tame your monkey mind.' According to a Buddhist Principle, as you feel your monkey mind going out of control, just concentrate, take a deep breath and focus.

"Focus is a muscle, and you can build it," you can improve your power of focus with your mindset. Use it as a tool that you can foster and use it in the most effective way possible. As a matter of fact, your survival depends upon how active you tackle the important things in your daily life. By mastering this ability to focus you can shift your thoughts to a more realistic spectrum. You have to change the way you view your chores and professional endeavors; you have to prepare your brain to pay attention to the things that really matter.

Calmly Prepare your Brain:

You have to calm your brain before you embark on any chore. With a deep breath and a comfortable posture approach your work with composure; you will have the desired concentration level within no time. If you maintain your mind in peace and tranquility you can make better decisions, feel more confident and focused on building your mental strength. Create a more relaxing environment at both homes and work to put your mind at ease.

Unplug Yourself:

You need to unplug yourself from on-line distractions such as emails, social media, smartphones, etc. You have to disconnect yourself from online life which is draining your brain. A few minutes are enough to recharge yourself by comfortably sitting at a quiet place, listening to tranquil music and doing easy exercises.

This is going to increase your productivity and involvement in your work.

According to a study, "Today's smartphone users check their phones 150 times a day, which is the equivalent of spending 2.5 hours a day just opening and closing the phone. A single text message, which takes approximately 2.2 seconds to read, can double error rates on basic tasks; even worse, workers find that it takes an average of 11 minutes to get back into the flow of the previous task. Our phones have become compulsions, rather than tools of efficiency."

That clearly shows how distracted our daily lives can be. You have to steer away from your distractions and stop your mind from being clouded over completely. Try to overcome your compulsions to pick up your phone while you are executing an important work task. Sometimes, all you need is some time with only you and your mind.

Avoid Focus Killers:

You need to avoid everyday focus killers which prevent you from performing at your fullest. Everyday stress and getting less sleep are very common focus killers, it can leave you out of focus and distract you in the worst kind of way. Other common focus killers are your smartphone notifications, Social Media engagements and the long list of unwanted emails in your inbox.

Your focus needs to be strained. It must be scheduled and segmented with what kind of work you have to do and how long it needs your attention. You have to be aware and mindful where you're emphasizing your focus. It is clever management of your immense focus and intense distraction.

Have some Coffee, fresh Fruits or Vitamin Juice:

If you want to boost your energy and ability to be attentive so grab a cup of coffee or a bowl of fresh fruits or a class of your favorite vitamin juice. Believe me, it is not just a break, the caffeine in the coffee, fresh seasonal fruits and a vitamin juice of your choice can actually make you more focused, mentally alert and revitalized.

Several studies verify that coffee is an attention booster. "In a study published in the Journal of Alzheimer's Disease, French physiologist Astrid Nehlig identifies a connection between caffeine and cognition. While caffeine doesn't improve learning or memory performance, Nehlig found it does increase physiological arousal, which makes you less apt to be distracted and better able to pay attention during a demanding task."

Tricking Your Brain:

You have to create tricks to deceive your mind to produce positive distractions which may lead to finish the task. We can use our brain effective by repeatedly sending signals that help it to be on track and leaves little room to be out of track. As we already know many psychiatrists have called our brain a muscle that can be improved while working regularly with different mental tasks. We can send targeted messages to our brains to work the way we want it to be.

Detaching from the Noise:

Noise is considered as one of the serious distractors which kill creativity and productivity at once. All you have to do is create a working environment with a complete absence of sound. The more peaceful of an environment you create the more conducive it would become to work with the utmost attention. The calm and composed working place is mandatory if you want to grow your productivity.

Breaking the Routine Cycle:

We have learned that routine is a killer and that is correct in many ways because following a routine certainly brings your productivity at stake. All you have to do is make our routines more diversified to get out of boredom. Daily repetitions of our routine work make your brain's ability to think slower. Even your mind needs change to work efficiently. You have to break the routine cycle by listening to music, by writing a creative context piece, by eating healthy, exercising and focusing on to meditate.

'The Being On-line' Syndrome:

Technology is the greatest distractions we have today. With smart gadgets always by our sides, we are becoming restless all the time and that is also the major source of losing our productivity. Every person is craving online presence and is being infected with the digital space given to them. In turn, decreasing productivity drastically. This dilemma is not too difficult to overcome if you prioritize your tasks smartly with a pragmatic approach and define what you use the technology for and then disseminate this message to your brain.

Avoid Boredom:

Boredom makes it difficult to work efficiently if not impossible; you have to streamline your work without getting fade up. Doing things differently and using positive distractors make your work interesting and get you out of boredom such as reading something interesting or listening to classical music or funny TV show would definitely be a good idea to boost your focus.

Productive people are not superhumans or sophisticated machines, but they are more disciplined and focused on their tasks. If you want to have real-life examples dig into the lives of super-productive people and try to learn how they take on their daily tasks, how they start their day, how they distribute different tasks into different segments, how they get most out of their workforce.

It is no more rocket science to reach the highest level of productivity, to achieve it you have to follow certain proven methods that lead you to the top.

You have to be more specific when you list your to-do-list. Your list of daily tasks should be precise. If it is a haphazard and confusing it will leave you in a state of disarray so make sure when you choose your tasks, be specific.

Set Realistic Goals:

Set your goals realistically after assessing your workforce and their ability to complete tasks. You have to adopt a pragmatic approach to achieve your goals with optimum productivity. For example, if your company has the potential to only produce 500 hundred products with the capacity of the workforce you have but you choose to set your goal to produce 1000 items in that specified time then that would be unrealistic. Make sure every time you set your goals you follow this principle. If not, it only releases an undue pressure on the workers. They should be given the leverage to do their job with their full capacity in a peaceful environment. By doing so high productivity would easily be achieved.

Have the Right Tools to Finish the Job:

Have the right Tools

You need to own the right tools in today's competitive business environment where every entrepreneur trying to find a niche competitive edge. Just provide the right tools like the machinery equipment or software programs required to render a certain task. You need to have them at the disposal so that there will be an increase in the productivity of your workforce.

Provide Excellent Work Conditions:

The provision of a proper workplace condition is a fundamental factor whenever you want a high-value product for your business place at any level. If your worker is at ease and in a state of mental peace, he or she would be willing to give their best. For example, if you are yourself a worker you will always want the best working conditions where you do not face any kind of distractions, which makes you focused and provide ignition to start your work without any hitches.

Automation:

Necessary automation is always needed when your goal is to achieve top-notch production at the workplace. Automation and its up gradation is a continual process as you diversify and add value to your products, you always need modern automation with state of the art tools to get the high-end results.

Time Management:

That goes without saying how important it is to manage time by assigning and dividing different time slots accordingly as per the requirement of your business. As it is said time is money and nothing is more precious than time, you have limited working hours to produce that's why Time Management plays a pivotal role in productivity.

Always make sure your employees are happy because without them you cannot do your business. If you want to increase your production with better quality and to achieve targets you have to make them even happier. Your workforce is the body & soul of your enterprise, give them incentives, give them breaks, give them a conducive working environment. If your work is unhappy you may find your targets unachievable and that is not good for your business.

Reward yourself sometimes and keep motivation intact:

Reward Yourself

Doing difficult tasks and sometimes accomplishing goals that are next to impossible, you should focus on rewarding yourself with a much-needed vacation or just throw a small party to enjoy time with your folks. You can even choose to go on a shopping spree if it makes you happy. Take this time for yourself and live in that moment because you deserve it and you have earned it.

Achieving unachievable targets drains your energy and leaves you in a state of mental and physical exhaustion; first and foremost, you should take a small break and have this time free from all pressures and hectic routines of daily work. Let's say go to the beach have fun and disconnect yourself for a while from all routine stuff, it freshens your brain and helps you re-gather yourself. by treating yourself with a nice reward. It is a proven fact that this kind of time outs make a new super-energized person of you who is ready to take up new challenges ahead.

At times, you are confused and you cannot find the source of your discomfort. Most of the time, what causes you discomfort while you work is your distracted mind. Since it is not in place, your thoughts become scattered. But never toss aside the beauty of productivity and hold it close to you.

CHAPTER 4:

CORRELATION OF FOCUS & SUCCESS

Focus leads to success and productivity

The goal of this chapter makes you understand the importance of concentration and focus when it comes to success. However, it is also necessary to know that you should be wiping sweat from your forehead for the goals that you truly desire. Currently, we live in a world that is advancing at a far greater speed than we initially signed up for. There is immense competition everywhere as doing even the simplest of tasks is becoming a nuisance. This is because people are rushing to make a mark in this world. As there are so many talented people out there who are achieving their ambitions, one feels left behind. And feeling left behind in this day and age is the same as being exposed to poisonous gas; it is painful and kills you in an instant. We are pushing ourselves to start something new and accept careers that we do not prefer.

All of it is to just earn a livelihood and conform to the shackles of capitalism. You end up tirelessly concentrating on goals that you never wanted to commit to, and it eventually leaves a bitter taste. As you grow up, you try to convince your children to take up the career that you couldn't. Then, they get stuck in the poisonous loop, all the while concentrating on the wrong goals. In the end, this compels them to get distracted quickly and indulge in leisure activities as that brings them the most comfort. Basically, to receive the true benefits of focus itself you need to focus on the right things; the things that you truly want to achieve.

Otherwise, you will end up losing your focus with the passage of time. However, if you do concentrate on the goals that you hold close, then nothing can stop you from climbing the staircase of success.

Why Focusing Can Also Go Beyond Just 'Completing A Task':

Before we talk about the correlation of focus and success, it is important to note the diversity of focus as well. It is the ultimate tool that you require to completely change your life and the decisions that you take. For example, Harry is a shy kid in school who is nervous enough to never speak up the answer in class even if he knows that it is correct. One day, there is a sports teacher that comes into the class to announce that there is a basketball competition happening soon. Suddenly, Harry realizes that he wants to participate because he used to play the sport back in elementary school. But he just cannot seem to raise his hand. He tries to figure out a solution to the problem mid-way. Then, he figures out that his internal fear of getting judged was stopping him from speaking his mind. He focused on his surroundings and thought of the different ways that he could be embarrassed. However, as he concentrated on the people around him, he understood that everyone was raising their hands. Yet, no one was visibly becoming the center of a joke or ridiculed. So, he believed that he could also do the same. Hence, he ended up raising his hand and got the chance to participate. You can continue on the story on your own now; probably give it a happy ending or something. But coming to the moral of the story, if Harry never focused on the problem that held him back then he could've never gotten the spotlight. When you focus, it helps you make a calculated decision rather than acting spontaneously. He wouldn't have raised his hand if he knew that a well-known bully was sitting in the class. If it weren't for focusing, he could've never either gotten to play basketball or probably would've just gotten humiliated. The pre-planned response on his part, which benefited him, was only possible because he didn't let his impulsivity take over him. And only employing the art of concentration can tackle the despairing nature of impulsivity.

Moreover, focusing also helps in silencing the evil voice in your head. In other words, when you focus you become self-aware which helps deal with negative thoughts. The thing is you cannot expect a negative thought to disperse as it appears in your head. The harder you try to push a particular thought away; it comes back with more intensity. It's like throwing a ball on a wall with hard force and then getting hit by the ball as it comes back with the exact same strength. You need to understand why you're having a negative thought and try to focus on it to originate its roots. Often, people calm down or panic knowing the reason for a particular thought. However, as the emotions subside, they realize that as they now know why they have the reoccurring thought, they can figure out a solution. It is the same as looking at your opponent's tricks during a match and avoiding future mistakes that could result in your loss.

Another thing that focus assists in is the concept of creativity. When you have the opportunity to focus on your surroundings, you are inspired because you're paying constant attention to everything. For example, you're supposed to be writing a book and you have to introduce a new character, which is a demon. As you start formulating the monster, you're confused over its shape and features. However, you lift your head to see the sky and get to see clouds of multiple shapes. When you keep observing you see that one of the clouds is shaped weirdly. So, you outline the cloud's shape to somehow make it fit the demon's description. Basically, when we keep focusing on a variety of things, it broadens our perspective. It fills up our creative juices and helps in developing things from scratch. This is the reason why artistic people are invested in their surroundings. They find comfort in observing and learning; which is only possible through retaining focus.

Talking about learning, focus also ensures that we get to expand our knowledge. Focusing is the ultimate method of controlling your mind to concentrate on almost anything. This brings us to the beginning of this chapter which mentions the importance of focusing on the 'right things'. Despite all of these benefits, not a lot of people get to profit from them. That's because we beat ourselves down over the 'negative' which is a very scary notion as you must've witnessed while reading the previous chapter. Though, moving along, you can comprehend why there is no time to be thinking like that as that slows our progress towards success.

Success and Focus – The Two Unmatchable Elements:

Have you wondered why so many motivational speakers are keen on talking about the art of concentration? The only mind that can ever taste success is the concentrated mind. When a person is focused then opportunities line up for them one by one. The reason is that focus is the best companion for achieving goals. For example, a child that is focused on his studies would eventually get good grades. This leads to a chain of positive events that include praise from parents or future scholarships. The path to positive opportunities opens up just like that. Even though, it isn't just a snap of a finger nor is it possible through praying, it requires patience and dedication. These two would be your best acquaintances during your journey to developing a concentrated mind.

Also, do not forget to take breaks in-between because without a little 'me time' it is impossible to practice focus. Even the infamous billionaire Bill Gates mentioned in his documentary 'Inside Bill's Brain' that he takes some time out of his life to think. He emphasized the importance of letting yourself go for a while and indulge in the process of thinking. There, Gates said that he comforted himself by reading books or papers. It served as a method of regaining himself back and helped him get back to work with a clearer mind. If even the greatest leaders of prominent companies need to step down and take a break, why shouldn't you? Giving yourself the privilege to slow down and ensure peace in your life is the utmost step required in the sequence of achieving focus. Here are some of the qualities that you can attain through remaining focused, which eventually leads to undeniable success:

Time Management

Moreover, no matter what you're trying to excel in, you have to focus anyways. All of the interesting inventions that benefit us were made from people that were unwilling to lose focus. Imagine if the person that worked on the cure of plague didn't realize the significance of his focus and just left the study mid-way. If we can owe these people so much, then we should also follow how they were determined to their work. The first thing that successful people don't waste is 'time'. They understand that time is the only factor that will not wait for them. They choose to use it wisely, making sure that they let out their creative thoughts on paper. It is for sure that you must've seen in movies how a writer or a scientist suddenly gets an idea, and they write it down. Why do they immediately put it to paper? This is because they know they can't dilly-dally as forgetting the idea with time is a huge possibility. They try to use their focus at the right time to give out an innovative idea that could be the next best thing! In the end, the focus is all about diverting your mind to the thing that matters the most.

Learning from Mistakes – How Planning Makes A Difference:

Furthermore, as you keep your focus straight, you'll sense that you don't mind going back to your mistakes and learning from them. A focused person is never afraid to tackle what set them back. They understand that learning and moving on is the best plan for improving. This is also the formula that successful people follow but they're only able to do so because they're focused. Hence, success and focus are like an unbreakable bond tied together like a red string of fate. You will never meet a fulfilled person talking about spending too much time on their mobile phone because successful people don't only focus but also plan. That is a point emphasized in the previous chapter as well. As you start making a defined plan that involves your goals as well as leisure activities, you can never hesitate. Think of it all as a maze. You can't get out of a maze if you just keep walking around aimlessly hoping that you can make it out somehow. But that is a behavior exhibited by a silly, unfocused person. You need to keep track of the blocked paths or make a map through the help of your mistakes to move forward. So, practically, you need to make a set plan that can help you focus on peace and avoid mistakes. Clever people understand this, which is why they rarely get overwhelmed by their surroundings. Even if there is a sudden change, their mind is trained to deal with it efficiently.

Lastly, the focus isn't an in-built quality, but it is nevertheless more than necessary. Its roots spread out to reach most aspects of life and have the potential to help with everyday decisions. The notion of leaving things for tomorrow is what is setting us apart from the population of winners. For example, you avoid doing your homework at a proper time and just aimlessly spend the first half of the day. Then, at night you have to sit through endless work while the other kids get to sleep or do other leisure activities. Focus is the reason why you're able to divide your time effectively. But once again, only focusing on the right things would help. It is always possible to divert your focus to useless concerns as well; this is why don't undermine your ability to focus. Use it as a strengthening tool to reel out success and join the league of the leaders. Then again, also remember to take breaks because if one of the world's richest men can take a break, you deserve a well-deserving break too. It is time to fight back the devil in your head that either convinces you to procrastinate or overwork yourself.

CONCLUSION

The impact of being distracted is huge; you may find yourself struggling to achieve high-end goals in your life. On the other side, if you do the opposite and succeed to develop a focus on your priorities, it places you on track. It is a constant battle inside and out; you have to make sure that you have to win every time whenever you face this standoff. By the time you start valuing your time, you have a complete vision of what you really want to go for.

The management of work and family life is the key to stay focus and be successful. You cannot afford to leave them at the cost of losing your shine in your family and work life. What you have to do is to behave intelligently. Make a plan stick to it break the cliché associated with all kinds of distraction. You have to balance every aspect of your life, distribute qualitatively. You also have to challenge the paradox of focus and success and convert the mystery behind into acclaimed accomplishment. Your response to every distraction should be calculated and professional.

Pay attention and try not to procrastinate it is just like you nip the evil in the bud. Do not postpone whether it is a long-term task or the short-term commitment do it now just as live the moment right now. It's an ongoing effort; you have to do it tirelessly to live your life according to your choices. For that matter, you have to draw a pragmatic plan that how you are going to achieve your lifelong goals, schedule everything, make a timeline.

Multitasking slows down your productivity, leave you out of focus, choose your tasks wisely and be fully attentive to them so as you finish them comprehensively. Prioritize every task on a daily basis and execute it with utmost focus, it is the key.

Create a bubble to protect yourself from technology ridden distractions such as Smartphones, Gaming apps, Notifications, Alarms, Emails, etc. disconnect yourself while you are doing your creative work. Be Offline for a while to gather your focus which is essential to finish your assigned job with authority. Listen to some soft music instead.

Meditation or prayer is a smart move if you are stuck in the middle of completing your task, meditation and prayer help ooze out pressures on body and mind exerted by your daily hectic life. Just take yourself easily and meditate or pray for a while not necessarily longer hours, just 20 minutes are enough. The wee hours of every morning are recommended to meditate or pray, they are best.

Small breaks in between can be quite impactful, like a nice coffee break. These breaks give you short term relief which helps re-energize yourself for long hours to handle the hectic workload. Besides that, coffee or tea provides you necessary caffeine, which is a brain stimulant too, hence it helps your brain work amazingly fast.

Once you equip yourself with healthy habits, both your mental and physical wellbeing will begin to flourish, and productivity increases as a result.

APPENDIX:

IMPLEMENTATIONS & TOOLS

Apply- Repeat- Succeed

You need to look after mental and physical potency to have it enough to improve your performance. Learning how to focus, perform better and build your capacity is essential to handle day to day distractions. If you learn to manage yourself physically and emotionally, then it is evident that you are ready for the big tasks to tackle.

Studies in brain research show that it takes 21 days of regular practice to get rid of toxic thoughts and to replace them with constructive, healthy ones. In order for it to become a new, deeply rooted positive thought pattern, it takes about 60 days of continuous practice. It begins by bringing the toxic thoughts from the subconscious mind into the conscious.

It is advisable not to change a multitude of patterns at once. Better pick one or two patterns and work on them focused, to attain the desired change throughout a 60-day period and once established, pick 1 or 2 other ones. This will lead to sustainable change and growth.

* * * * *

"Most people have no idea of the giant capacity we can immediately command when we focus all of our resources on mastering a single area of our lives."

Tony Robbins

Distraction Levels:

Identify the level of distraction in various situations in your daily life context.
Rate from 1 (very distracted) to 10 (highly focused):

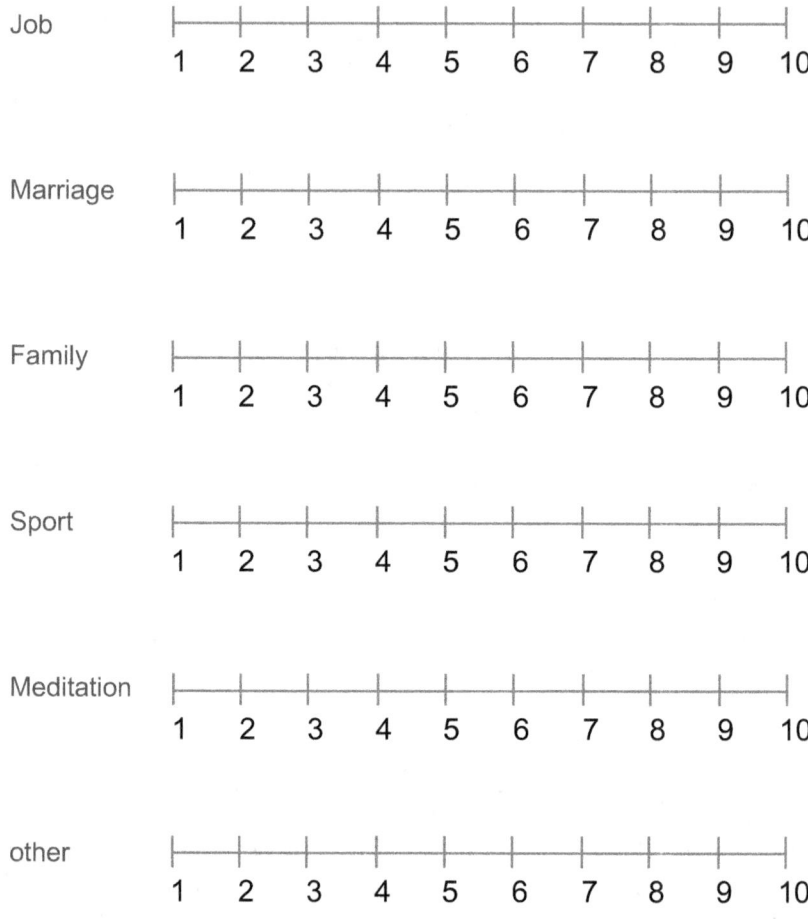

Job

      1   2   3   4   5   6   7   8   9   10

Marriage

      1   2   3   4   5   6   7   8   9   10

Family

      1   2   3   4   5   6   7   8   9   10

Sport

      1   2   3   4   5   6   7   8   9   10

Meditation

      1   2   3   4   5   6   7   8   9   10

other

      1   2   3   4   5   6   7   8   9   10

=> What does that tell you?
=> In which area of your life are you most distracted?
=> Why?
=> Was this always like this?

Internal Distraction Overcomer:

For a couple of days or weeks carry a notebook along and write down all the distracting thoughts as soon as they appear. This helps to identify the distracting thoughts, bring them from the subconscious to the conscious mind and helps find toxic and distractive thought patterns.

Once identified, start to remove them and replace with positive thoughts.

Example:
Identified thought: (written down in your notebook)

"I'm not good enough to do this job. This is frustrating, let me find some release of the inner pain by scrolling through social media."

Way to overcome:

Renounce this thought as a lie. Write down: "I'm capable of providing an excellent result. I now concentrate on the task at hand and reward myself once I'm done with this task."

External Distraction Remover:

Make a list with all your external distractions and define a way to tackle each one of them.

Distraction	Action to take	comments
Incoming SMS notifications	Turn off SMS notifications	
Constant incoming emails	Define 3 specific times a day to check and work through emails	
Picking up stuff on my work desk	Remove clutter, place all objects in cupboards or behind me out of sight	
Incoming phone calls interrupting my workflow	use answering machine during times of focused work	
...		
...		

=> Revisit your list and action plan every week.
=> Add new external distractions and define ways to tackle them.
=> Celebrate the ones you have overcome! Well done!

Procrastination Roots:

1. Identify your areas of procrastination and write them down.

----

2. Find out why you procrastinate in those areas?

----

3. What is the reason for it? (fear, brain wiring, boredom, inferiority, etc.)

----

4. What is the root cause? (upbringing, burn-out, lack of self-worth, etc.)

----

5. What do you try to avoid or achieve through procrastinating?

----

6. Do you need help to uproot? (Coach, Medical Doctor, Psychiatrist, etc.)

Goal Setting:

Write down your three main goals for this year.
Break them down to each month and each week.
=> Having long- and mid-term goals help tremendously focusing on the daily activities

Planning:

Plan the coming week at the end of the previous week or on Sunday night.
Plan the next day always the day / evening before.

Fillers & Drainers:

We all have different things that energize us, as well as things that drain all our energy. Stuff we love doing and others we hate. We all have a kind of an "Energy Tank". The fillers must exceed the drainers.
No one can only do the things he loves in life. Over the long run however, about 75% of the things that we do in life need to be in the "Filler" category in order to not run empty.

"Fillers"	"Drainers"
trail running	conflicts
reading books	precise detailed work
a glass of wine	long phone calls
deep conversations	
tackling challenging tasks	
...	...
...	...
...	...
...	...

Make your own list with your personal "Fillers" and "Drainers".
Are you balanced?
If you run too long on "empty" you won't be able to focus. Your productivity level will decrease and you risk ending up in a burnout.

Level of Productivity:

Map out your personal hours of different productivity levels in your daily schedule.

Colour in:
=> red: hours of low energy / productivity levels
=> yellow: hours of medium energy / productivity levels
=> green: hours of high energy / productivity levels

0 am	
1 am	
2 am	
3 am	
4 am	
5 am	
6 am	
7 am	
8 am	
9 am	
10 am	
11 am	
12 am	
1 pm	
2 pm	
3 pm	
4 pm	
5 pm	
6 pm	
7 pm	
8 pm	
9 pm	
10 pm	
11 pm	
12 pm	

=> When are your most fruitful hours of the day?
=> Do they match with your work routine in a positive way?
=> Do you make use of your most productive hours for important tasks?
=> Do you protect those hours from distractions?
=> Do you work on routine tasks during low energy level hours?
=> How can you adjust and improve your daily routine based on this new insight?

Food Patterns:

List your healthy and your unhealthy food habits => what am I going to consolidate and what are my steps of change / improvement

Healthy food habits:		
Positive habit	Action to take	comments
I regularly drink water	Keep doing it	
I eat fresh fruits three times a day	Keep doing and increase to 4 times	
...		
...		
...		
...		

Unhealthy food habits:		
Negative habit	Action to take	comments
I often eat chocolate when I'm stressed	Replace chocolate with a carrot, fruit or use chewing gum	
I often eat junk food	Eating whole-grain food and salad regularly	
...		
...		
...		
...		

Be intentional in keeping good habits and replace the bad ones with alternative products.
Read books, blogs and articles about healthy diets for maximum performance.

Automation

Take some intentional time to brainstorm for ways on how you could automatize tasks in your context (work, family, hobby, daily life, business, etc.)

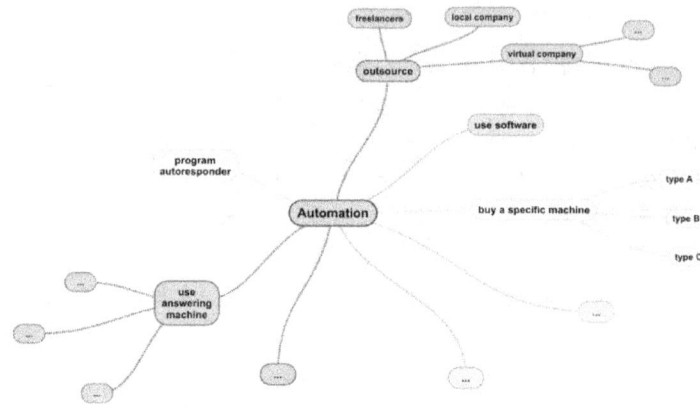

=> Then have other people add to your ideas
=> Select the best option and implement until successful

Personal reflections and lessons learned:

Write down your five key learnings out of this book:

1.

2.

3.

4.

5.

Write down three actions steps: "I will ..."

1.

2.

3.

Final Note

I believe you enjoyed every useful tool and self-help information read in this book.
The application of these valuable nuggets will help you begin to experience a more organized life and tremendous progress in all you do.

If this book was helpful for you and you liked it, kindly give it a ☆☆☆☆☆ Five Star rating and a compelling review to help others see and want to read this life-transforming book.

If you have any feedback or proposals to improve or extend the content of this book, or suggested themes for a follow-up book, let me know at: focus2thrive.now@gmail.com

Overcome Distractions – Be Focused – Increase your Productivity and enjoy Life to the fullest...

Yours
David Turner

"Let us know your opinion, we treasure your feedback!"

www.ingramcontent.com/pod-product-compliance
Lightning Source LLC
Chambersburg PA
CBHW070517220526
45467CB00002B/707